T0001059

PEBBLE SWING

Pebble Swing

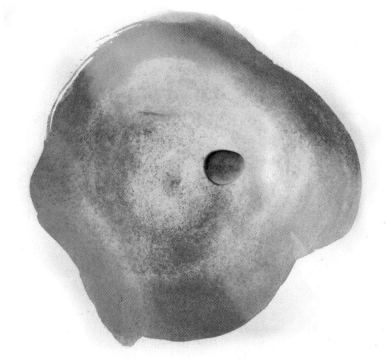

Isabella Wang

NIGHTWOOD EDITIONS | 2021

Copyright © Isabella Wang, 2021

1 2 3 4 5 — 25 24 23 22 21

ALL RIGHTS RESERVED. No part of this publication may be reproduced, stored in a retrieval system or transmitted, in any form or by any means, without prior permission of the publisher or, in the case of photocopying or other reprographic copying, a licence from Access Copyright, the Canadian Copyright Licensing Agency, www.accesscopyright.ca, info@accesscopyright.ca.

Nightwood Editions
P.O. Box 1779
Gibsons, BC VON IVO
Canada
www.nightwoodeditions.com

COVER DESIGN: Angela Yen
TYPESETTING: Carleton Wilson

Canada Council   Conseil des Arts
for the Arts   du Canada

BRITISH COLUMBIA
ARTS COUNCIL

BRITISH
COLUMBIA

Nightwood Editions acknowledges the support of the Canada Council for the Arts, the Government of Canada, and the Province of British Columbia through the BC Arts Council.

This book has been produced on 100% post-consumer recycled, ancient-forest-free paper, processed chlorine-free and printed with vegetable-based dyes.

Printed and bound in Canada.

LIBRARY AND ARCHIVES CANADA CATALOGUING IN PUBLICATION

Title: Pebble swing / Isabella Wang.
Names: Wang, Isabella, author.
Description: Poems.
Identifiers: Canadiana (print) 20210244704 | Canadiana (ebook) 20210244747 | ISBN 9780889714069 (softcover) | ISBN 9780889714076 (HTML)
Classification: LCC PS8645.A5317 P37 2021 | DDC C811/.6—dc23

TO SCOUT

for words said and words we knew without needing to say.

For this is the morning, the beginning of light.
For this is love, the season for things to grow.

—Simin Behbahani

CONTENTS

IV: Hindsight

I

I remember

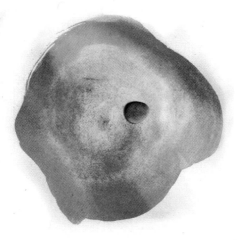

THIS WINTER IN GASTOWN

315 Carrall Street. A scarf around my neck.
This portion of Gastown Christmas-perfect,
you can almost imagine Tiny Tim next corner down.
The fashion boutiques I browse
with my eyes, faux furs flashing rhinestones
on collars, jewellers selling vintage keepsakes,
but I have no one to give them to. This season
I do not know how to celebrate the holidays.

The Victorian architecture stands from 1867
as Gassy Jack had left his own tavern, right down
to the cobblestones, to the horse-drawn carriage
running through this triangular peninsula at night.
The millennials are having avocado toast
on sourdough, Americano on drip with foam
extra frothy. The fingers of lovers interlocking
over wool-knit mittens. Look up.
Feel the warm glow of these coloured lights
casting from rooftops and lampposts.

Do you know what it feels like to be swallowed
by constellations, like stars? Imagine Annie
skipping down Victory Square singing "Tomorrow."
We glimpse ourselves before storefront windows,
picturing our reflections like those of families
gathered, their laughter spilling like cheese fondue
over charcuterie, a single green olive in the martini glass.
This winter when we marvel at laughter, joy—
an endless montage that some have managed
to replicate with their lives as in the movies,
we, too, will be moved to tears.

BURNED OUT

Dad came. He brought with him
a tree this time and ornaments
but forgot the star
so our fake spruce from Jining
with its crumpled-up tinsel
seemed kidnapped from the forest.

I spent the day in my closet, a makeshift hideout
with a pillow, a few blankets,
lamp where the sweaters used to go.
Nestled in a valley of unfolded clothes strewn
about on hangers like vines in a jungle,
I ventured out of my lair
only for a bread roll and more cranberry juice.

Locked away
with the latest TV episodes streaming
on Netflix, or whatever Christmas special they've got.
No traces of the outside world but daylight
seeping through the cracks
until I covered those too.

Pictures of my friends
at the light festival in Van Dusen,
a selfie my best friend took around a Christmas tree
with streaks of blue and purple lights
tagging everyone but me.
They had asked me to come.
Got a date with a carton of ice cream
and some mini bagels.
They thought I was joking.

Apparently it snowed outside, but I never noticed.
The ice killed two people
heading home along the Burrard Street Bridge
as I dozed off for a nap at seven p.m.
The Audi R8 motorist who collided
with the sixty-eight-year-old taxi driver
and his passenger
went up in flames with the car.
I tried picturing myself, a bystander
at the scene, warming my hands.
Where else do you go on a night like this
for warmth? The coffee shops were closed.
Snow fell, but the embers persisted.
I thought about showing my friends the article
but it would ruin the mood.

I kept scrolling
pausing to stare at a picture of a Yorkshire terrier
and heard my own whimpering
for affection. It's been days
since I took the puppy out for a walk.
I fed him the last of my bread roll and headed out
in pyjamas and flip-flops, praying
the neighbours wouldn't recognize me in the dark.

ELEGY FOR WINTER

Thawing, I want to be the announcer of good news.
    I want to be the boughs of maple trees,
the arms of children that, like trees, elevate their limbs

upon first sight of snow. I want to be the invitation
    that conducts inches of the sky's
infinitesimal flowers to us each year, or assume

the receiving end as the ground, grooming
    its birthmarks with the ritual frost
of winter's exhale. I want to be an infinite pattern

of snow crystals greeting a child's morning wishes,
    to be the granter of wishes in as many
diverse branches as snow. There's an inspiring beauty

to snow I'm beginning to see again—
    something about earlier drafts of a poem
I wrote in winter, that I felt the need to transform afterward—

unlearn the unlearning, unbreak what had been broken.
    I know there is a lot of hurting in the world
right now. I know it's difficult to hear another poem

about grieving. So I want to be a lot of things good
    and maybe the snow does too. Maybe that's why
it clings on to our mittens. Maybe it wants to feel

the warm comfort of wool. Be that comfort
    to strangers, the twine that knits itself
around the negative spaces of longing and marrow

where fingers and bones are still rummaging
    for explanations. I had a dream
where it snowed for three days, and the snow melted.

When I woke up, I knew it might not snow
    again this year. It might be fruitless hanging on
to old poems, trying to revive my memories

of a lost winter. As if plucking out the tulip bulbs
    I immersed in the garden last fall
would somehow make the frozen soil

in my palms bloom again, a poem
    where the only feeling it exuded
onto the reader the first time was brokenness—

what if I were to say to the world, *Look,*
    you are changing so fast. You are so broken
I can't follow you.

Is your snow a metaphor
    for the thawing
that began

before you were ready to know?

LUNAR FEAST

1. A tanka

As other families sit
to feast at this year's table,
I overindulge
on the spring rolls and nian gao
wafting out of their windows.

2. Year of the dog

My mother made dumplings for the dog today.
Flour and water embraced to dough,

a handful of dog kibble ground with a mortar and pestle,
carrots and celery chopped to a fine pulp.

Dad and I waited in the other room to the sound
of rolling pin against cutting board, floured dough

scraping hardwood as she kneaded.
The filling nursed between tips of two silver chopsticks,

stack of paper-thin disks rolled—she cupped them
in her hand the way you cup a red lotus

at the Lunar Parade
each year to make a wish.

Two fingers dipped into water, edges sealed
with neat folds.

With dogs, she says, *you just need to feed them
and they remain grateful forever.*

Dad and I went for a stroll in the neighbourhood.
Around us, upside-down banners and red lanterns.

Fruit for luck. Tangyuan, dusted in flour, filled
with sweetened sesame, peanut or red bean paste—

served from bamboo baskets with each glutinous
rice ball nudged tightly beside the other

in a circle, like family members gathered by the round table.
In the year to come, they are to bring harmony and unity.

Noodles with mustard greens for longevity,
tossed with spring onions and chili in peanut sauce.

Spring rolls for wealth. Steamed fish in ginger and soy sauce
for abundance. Sticky nian gao for progress.

We considered waiting out the evening, ringing
the doorbells and asking for their leftover tangyuan

and maybe spring rolls. Instead, we gorged
on these smells that will satiate us for another year.

GHAZAL FOR A SNOW DAY ON THE MOUNTAIN

Snow scraping the bough of a bent oak tree, in it a hummingbird's nest
abandoned, made of moss and soft plume fibres cupped in snow.

When was the last time I've been back home? The cherry tree stands
no more a sapling than I am a child. Let it blossom before spring melts
    the snow.

The wind chimes kept me awake as I dreamt a poem about highways.
Wind chimes through trees. Outside, sound of a shovel clearing snow.

The janitor starts her shift after the buses have stopped running.
Sign on the university building reads, *Library closed due to the snow.*

Like dandruff falling, salt crystals scaling the bare maple tree: a life
I've only imagined as the inner decorum of some broken snow globe.

GHAZAL FOR HEIRLOOM FAMILY RECIPES

My grandmother taught me five different ways to deflesh a bitter gourd,
how to scrape off the residue left from seeds so it would taste less bitter.

Recipe for old-fashioned liquor: Replace the sugar cube with elderberries.
In an ice-filled mixing glass, stir bourbon, St. Germain and bitters.

The best coffee was served to me by a young woman at the Ethiopian café—
it was sweet on its own, and permeated all the necessary tinges of bitterness.

When you leave water in a cup for too long, it evaporates. Can't say
the same about honey, but it's beginning to clump. Tea leaves turn bitter.

My grandfather died while eating crab and red wine—heart attack.
This is a spell we are currently under, but I promise it won't stay bitter.

GHAZAL FOR MY GRANDMOTHER

She forgets to close the curtains on the day I leave. Her eyes trail
my back—two blocks to the street curb where I turn, never letting go
   of the curtains.

The purple vase on the kitchen counter sits without flowers. We leave it
   there to collect dust.
My pupils are so dark they scare her, absorb light in through the curtains.

At the hospital where she does her intake, they hand her a blue gown
that exposes her back. She comes out a different woman from behind
   the curtains.

I grind the pills in her food—she can't swallow. That evening,
she soils the bed again. There are no more comforters, so I remove one
   of the curtains.

I'll be back from school. She doesn't seem to hear me.
She stays in the same spot, brightened from being on this side of the
   daffodil curtains.

REDEMPTION

He didn't want another mouthful
of boiled tree bark. Nothing his grandmother
did or said could calm him.
She tried rocking him,
beating him, stripping him naked
and leaving him to bask red in the snow.

She dug out a jar of meat curing
underground for the New Year's,
scooped marinated veal from the salty brine
mixed with braised cabbage
and the last of their rice for the winter,

served it to him head bowed—a peace
offering to an angry god. One year
before she passed, my father
bought her train tickets
to the city, presented her with roasted
duck, lamb stew, ginseng tea.

No more teeth left, she sucked
on shards of greasy skin
dipped in oyster sauce,
drawing flavour before spitting
out the gloopy chunks.

And he sat and watched
as she wrapped what she had spat
in bits of tissue, stuffing
them down her pant leg pockets
to save for later.

I REMEMBER

after Joe Brainard

I remember   it takes more than one person to remember
That's why the word has
     member in it—
a vestigial of thought, or a collective

I remember   a time and a land and the process of forgetting
     that wasn't any time
or land I've resided in my lifetime
     but I remember   because the women
in my family had stories

     I remember   stories
     as a kind of land you arrived at
And I remember   poetry
as both an immigration policy   and the destination that was a city
wrote me

I remember
     continents as rock formations with history
     And   some histories
too loud for young ears to hear
     and that's why my parents said we were leaving

I remember   leaving ours behind
but not the leaving

     The poetry of Li Bai
     clearer than any language   that has been
     bestowed upon me

I remember   being told that it took six months
for a letter he wrote to arrive by sea
        and the thick scrolls of watercolour paintings
                with red emblems in a cursive I could not read

And I remember   fishermen
        who risked their lives
for a couple of stamped copper coins
to deliver the words of the country's poets in ink

        I remember   reading the Pinyin of 静夜思
in grade one, Li Bai's poem
        about how a person glimpsing the rays of moonlight
missed his ancestral homeland

                I folded down the ear of the accompanying image
                from the book:
blue, on top of water
like a salty river that wept the colour of sadness

I remember   land as river you can excavate
I remember   the children and their villages
and jujube trees
and schools with plastic bags for windows
and laps for desks
and jasmine-flavoured incense lit with the corner of their little red
    books of Mao's writing

I remember   construction workers
pouring cement down our extinguished fictions

Land reclaimed
and the future of the country's children
            revised under a new ideology

I remember   my father's childhood ingrained in a patch
of jujube trees
            by the front entrance
of his village's elementary school—
            that his mother
helped to establish
                        planted the trees with her students

I remember   the dirt-lined rims of his tiny thumbs grasping
the edges of Mao's little red book

            The structure of the day's lecture
                counting more fingers and toes you've lost
than you have left   from frostbite on the four-mile walk
            to first class

        I remember   road as metaphor
                    for river and its significance to me

            The curvature of the schoolyard
        behind which was a wood
                    with jujube trees and a stream
I remember   my father
as the "No-Mom" kid the village knew

            Wanting to be with him on the trees planted
            by his mother,
        his seventh year where he'd imagine himself being
hugged and carried by her

But when nobody was looking
into the trees he would shout
But what were
you like   Mother ? ? ?

I remember   the land on which
my grandmother
was seized by the Chinese Communist Leader
I remember   her life reclaimed
like water that fed the village children
buried   and lost forever

I remember land
as the body   and hug   and whisper   and mother of my father
and grandmother   I never knew

Therefore I remember   land
as a body of poems   I carved into the ground
with a stick
and turned to mud with the tears of my father

I remember   my father who never intended to tell me any of this

I remember asking him
about this grandmother I never knew
He said, *Your nai nai gen yei yei zhu zai*
shan li mian, how jiu mei jian ni le

And I said, *No, tell me about your other mother*
Your mother mother
I remember   his reaction:
How do you know about her?

I remember   the landing and the years
          the growing up and the rain that wore Vancouver as cologne.

          I remember   two years after becoming a writer
     the latest poem a collection of letters   to my grandmother
               I never knew

     I remember   a poem entitled "Dear Nan,"
          the part of the poem where I asked her
May I call you that?

     And thinking it a historical tragedy
that the words for the names of family members are given
but no one had ever given me *her* name

          I remember   Tiananmen Square—the panorama
               overlooking tower gates
Chang'an Avenue a stretch of road
en route to school
                    intersecting two districts
          This square I remember
clearer than the contours
                    of my grandmother's face

     But I remember   the heart of the archive
like a nineties reel-to-reel tape
          my country could never erase
          because the women in my family still had their stories

I remember   opening and shutting the windows
of our rented bedroom in a house on 41st   one minute
you were a part of the streets below   the next
                              all was silent

I remember   many afternoons, collecting fallen chestnuts
                and the crinkling layers of   rotten leafy mush
                    swimming in it as if I was in water

I remember   going to see the salmon run in the Okanagan
            learning of the gruelling journey
            that the parents had to endure
before spawning and dying

                I remember looking at the distance we've crossed
            and the distance a poem
still has to voyage to make it in   translation

            I remember the going back   and the returning
And the going back that never happened   And the story of one
of Li Bai's poems
on the other side of translation

                that once there   forgot its roots and mother tongue
            and the fact that it had prior origins at all

On days when the task of translation becomes too great
        I remember   forgetting the fact
that the members   of my family have forgotten me

29

ON FORGETTING A LANGUAGE

I started choreographing in my head again
though it's been two years since
I've danced, and the calluses between my toes
have grown tender. My feet have widened
from lack of restraint, my body
no longer responds under command to
chaîné, détourné, développé
like second nature, like a head turning
toward Grandmother's call
every time the telephone rang.

The studios I left behind shunned me
more than my own family did
when I couldn't remember
their faces, their names, how to write
my own name, how to write our language.
My grandmother doesn't know why I refuse to see her.
I don't know what my language *is* anymore.

After every class I lay on the ground
rooting myself in the studio's sprung wooden floors.
Back sticky from sweat and rosin,
legs raised to the barres where I let them hang.

I ordered a shipment of fifty pointe shoes
and pounded their tips thin.
When they said, *You must feel the ground with your feet,*
it was pain you felt. Pain
was how you connected to the ground
and at home, I shared it with others.

Quitting ballet isn't like forgetting
my first language. Now my family will not
talk to me and I reach for the studios
once more, to the place I learned to express
words I could not say
as sharp, fluid lines honed against music.

Every once in a while, I try to force
new blubber into old leotards,
gel my greasy hair back into a tight bun,
enunciate my name in Chinese
just to get a feel of what it was once like.

If I return to my birthplace, Jining, now
I will return as a foreigner
like the time I stepped onto this land ten years ago
as a Chinese immigrant
and realized there was no place
for my language in this new country.

II

The last sketch of a retracting spring

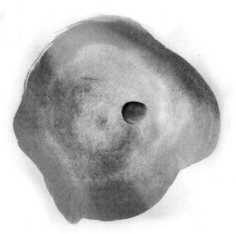

SPRINGTIME GHAZALS

I

The colour of plum blossoms taints my dreams.
Light turns the wallpaper.

Time falls in gradients down the hourglass—
Tlick... Tlock... Tlick... Tlock...

The mechanic heartbeat
                of a petal falling.

In my dreams, the deceased shadow
of a country laid to rest.

I, Isabella, was born to a cradle full
of tempest rains, the white flower in blooms.

*

The rhododendron an explosion of blooms
where a dog peed last winter—pink before, now blue.

A parcel arrives wrapped in blue flax paper
with the word *coda.*

The silhouette of the bird shudders, then falls
from behind closed shutters.

Souvenir from my mother's trip to Africa:
seven ivory elephant figurines.

Tell me, does it hurt the ground more or the tree
if you are to extract it by its roots?

*

III

Again today, someone has asked me where I am from.
I am of this earth.

My mother's womb, I say. Plum blossoms
don't fall on a late Sunday morning. It's spring cleaning.

Each day I aspire to be more like water.
The kind that can be reached into, and still flow.

I leave an armchair out in the back alleyway.
Then, I leave myself out.

We wait for dusk to fall.
Like driftwood, waiting. To be softened by the rain.

*

IV

Thin scrolls of rice paper
placed before me: a topography of Asia.

I practise blotching my first ink characters
in Chinese, turning ripples into tears.

A map disintegrates
with the stroke of a fine horsehair brush. A holy place—

the tombed basilica of Sheshan
where I looked with my father for the last time.

Beyond the one-way curvature
of a railway track, I am chugging out of China.

Only a plum blossom emerges—the reified outlines
of a country I once called home.

*

V

Dwindling candle, ticking flame.
The plum blossoms are burning.

Light remains in the closed shutters
of my eyelids.

Autumn sunshine pulls through
the rim of a glass mug.

A robin appears
from the last sketch of a retracting spring.

Here, it's morning. Not where she is.
My grandmother is dying.

And I, am in full bloom.

*

EXPECTING

I arrive as a frisson of vomit rising
to rust her throat. Pith growing
in the marshy confines of her belly
tethered to her navel
and our game of tin-can telephone.
I kick, she rubs.
Ba Ba lays down his head
and hears me tremor,
plays Beethoven from the other end.

Her blood tests anemic.
She is fed racks of Szechuan lamb,
fish stew, won ton soup,
uncooked oysters and chamomile
tea by Grandmother,
gags back six hard-boiled eggs
and a whole watermelon each day.

The midwives judge her size,
joke to the obstetrician
that four of us will transpire
in the delivery room.
Ye Ye demands a grandson
bearing his own name.

She gains sixty pounds. I come out
a shrivelled prune and hairless,
red as a blood orange. Dying chick
ringed by a chorus of watchful vultures,
threaded to an IV for refusing
water and infant formula.

They are generous with their gifts
and pleasantries, donate old comforters
for diapers. I wear Lao Lao's
hand-stitched socks and sweater.
Our family will finally have a doctor!
Here's money for a piano!
All little girls should take ballet class!
I love her toes! Ye Ye leaves.

Face puffy and porous
like a pomelo with dewy eyes,
Mama trains my body, furls me
in a blanket rolled so tight
there will be no room for mistakes.

THIS IS SPRING

The petals of wild cherry blossoms—
ying hua—bleed by the warmth of my hands.
In my hand, a gorge erupts
to fill the calligraphy
of the earth's expanding frame.
From between the meadow and the Clark's nutcracker
perched on a raft, it opens—
opens and closes to weave together
the contrapuntal elements of our terraformed song.

Another winter has gone, the late season.
Tiger lilies remodel by the fragrance
of vanilla and honey—
my cousin's sweet coconut bun
oozing with lemon meringue cream.

A red toboggan leans
by the side of a stump from seven winters ago.
Before leaving for China,
my cousin takes me to a Chinese diner
so I will remember.

You can season fried pickerel
with soy sauce, she demonstrates,
down the orifice of the fish's gnathic bone—
this trick, taught to her
by the women in my family
because I headed West.

My skirt, torn by the brambles
of a blackberry bush
as we say goodbye.
Hei mei, she mouths the words.

Hei mei—blackberries.
The Pinyin not unlike English,
so I can still pronounce
the words on the edge of my tongue.
The berries still hard—I squeeze,
staining the topography of her palms red.

LATE

For Kris Ma

Everything's late this year.
Nothing's dissolved since my last visit to Waterloo—
an evening at the park staring at geese,
my childhood friend and I taking turns
pushing each other on swings,
pretending we are children.
I walk him to his dorm, low moan
of the elevator rails grinding
as we wave goodbye, steel door
sliding shut between us.

Another ice storm strikes
and it's snowing again.
In Waterloo they call it a second winter.
I call to check if he's still alive,
send recipe links for udon and mujadara,
YouTube instructions
of someone cutting an onion.
He texts me back weeks later
saying I need to chill—
It wasn't really a storm,
just regular rain with a bit of wind and ice.

Here in Vancouver—sun and snow
at a standstill, scent of cropped
grass and gasoline in the rain. Flakes
of cherry blossoms bloom
and fall to dust barren sidewalks.
The blackbirds resolve to nest on lampposts.

The kitchen smelled like burnt manure
the day a van mowed
twenty-six sidewalk pedestrians
in Toronto. I left sage leaves in the oven
for too long. The news shrugs off misogyny,
labels suspect as mentally ill,
a man not loved by enough women.

They say there are still good people in the world.
Ten dead. Seats offered on subways,
a man stoops to collect groceries
spilling out of a woman's bag.
Strangers wish each other good night.

He texts me good night
from Waterloo, sends me
our favourite emoji, the blue fish,
tells me there is talk of peace:
the North and South
Korean leaders shook hands.

My parents lose custody of a red alder
to our neighbour whose son
smokes marijuana
on the porch every night, threatens
to kick my dog's head off
if it doesn't shut up. Bare branches
stick out in the neighbourhood
like thick cobwebs in the ripening heat of May—
the tree would not bud.
I watch them remove it from my bedroom window,
the bird's nest falling.

It's spring. Dad still hasn't come back.

SYNAPSES AND GRASS

一

grass   grass   grass
grass   grass   grass   grass   grass

      fish in the river

the innards of a tree
can't remember what species there was
that grew in Yongdong Village

an egg
on his grandfather's fiftieth birthday

a bowl of fermented meat
and vegetables in a jar dug from under
his grandparents' land

fifty grains of rice
told to count them out   rinse
boil   divide into three

all my father had to eat in a year

二

in my country   fifty years ago
little boys were trained
to play soldier
my father sculpted the shell
of a gun from mud

the sound of bullets
they made with their mouths

the red guards   ushering past
my father's cradle
a memory file   then grand nai nai

was gone   she took with her
a picture of the sky   the sky

        like impact
wounds
to the head   my father's shame

                        became my obsession

what he refused to talk about
lined my bookshelves

三

complete the puzzle
synapse after synapse after synapses
         break your father's
memory   apart

how will you piece

yourself together

one after one   after one   steps

toward home   later

    the road led nowhere

but the walk was very long

PEBBLE SWING

How do you grieve something you never really loved to begin with?
—Natalie Lim, "Arrhythmia"

I went on a fishing trip
to that part of yourself where no one goes.

To the knee-high busting brim
of surface water, where the *you* you think you are

counts the number of times
you can pebble swing

before empty syllables hit your reflection
like a lakeside wishing well's wane.

Yes, I've gone horribly off-tune,
but Natalie, a kite only stays afloat for so long.

*

I once wrote with a green metallic marker
on my wrist, 我, *me*—

The only word in Mandarin
I knew, I tried to wipe it off with acid.

If I approach the homeless folks here,
some won't take my money.

They say, *Go back
to where you are from.*

But Natalie, I've lost that deeper
pronunciation in my voice to find my way back.

*

Natalie, there's a kind of music that persists
long after the pianist has left the stage.

People here still ask me where I'm from,
but if I say China they won't believe me.

The way people look at me
when I walk out of fine dining in Chinatown.

The man selling spiced fish and ginkgo
at the pharmacy still talks to me in Chinese.

So I pebble swing to your footsteps,
the shuffle-rhythm of you walking up behind me.

*

Even as I say it now, 我, *wǒ*—it's as a local would.
The kids here tried burying me once

under the wayward swing
of buildings from construction sites.

So I tried to annihilate
my own language from inside of me.

Synaesthesia appears to me now
as music from traffic lights. Proverbial phrases.

The pebbles swing back by themselves.
I cast them out, and they keep coming back.

*

Natalie, I lied when I said I wasn't capable
of feeling.

I don't miss the country I left behind, a language
I will never read—*No, I'm sorry, this story is a lie.*

I am two lovers occupying a single strand
of music. Hard like rubies.

But Natalie, there's a song in the skyline
where the roosting birds feed.

I'm still waiting for the hummingbirds
to find me—take me, take me.

In this hand are no passions,
except the symphony I've denied myself of hearing.

*

LAYING ROOTS

for Ashley Hynd

First breakfast since moving to a place of my own.
Coffee in a press, peanut butter on waffles,
stack of back issues piled higher than the railings
I lean on to watch the man across the back lane,
naked from the waist up, sipping mojitos.

I wrapped the rocks you gave me in green cotton cloth,
carried them on the plane back from Waterloo
to twenty-four-hour cafés and street curbs where
I spend my nights thinking about people far away.

Amethyst, a soothing purple to relax me.
Bloodstone to revive me, offer courage and protection.
Carnelian for when I have writer's block—months of no poems
when I'm afraid to call myself *poet*
for much longer. Petrified wood—from the Greek *petro*
"wood turned into stone"—for laying roots, which I'm doing now.

You gave me unakite, pink within green,
harbouring love and kindness, which you taught me.

I've laid them on my bedside table knowing I can stay,
knowing I can place them down and not fear
losing them. Because when I'm full of fear and panic
petrified wood is said to bring me safety,
ground me here in my new home where you are always welcome.

MOTHER EXPLAINS MEN

You thought she'd be happy
now that you are doing fine.
This past summer in bed,
you pictured yourself falling
out of an open window
to nowhere—your first summer
spent away from home.
She said she wouldn't watch you
throw your future away,
waste seventeen years of
thankless upbringing
on the impracticalities of writing.
If you are going to do it, she says,
leave. So you did.

And anyway, she tells you,
you'll never find work as a writer.

Now you have four jobs
and she tells you to quit them,
says you'll fall behind in school,
that *No men will want to date you*
if they see how you write
about your parents.

Not that you are capable
of having intimate relationships
with anyone—you've tried.
She's the one who made you
emotionally scarred—
you want to tell her that.

Instead, you say over the phone,
Great, I'll date queer then.

BALCONY

To be a part of summer rain
and be sheltered, to share
a meal on the balcony
with a friend, to have company
for the first time since I've moved here.

To have birds that wake me,
a wood white butterfly touring the fence,
a tenant who waters the garden
every morning and tends to pot
growing in a pot,
morning dew lined on clotheslines
like strings of pearls,
I'm never lonely.

We share Bombay potatoes
and my first successful attempt
at mujadara after eight failed tries,
citrus steeped in green tea,
poured over ice. Earlier that day,
I took a cutting knife
to the lettuce leaves
growing in the garden,
being sure not to scrape the stem.

Soon, tomatoes will blush
under the heat. We'll harvest them
with the potatoes and squash,
toss them with seasoned onions,
from dirt to oven
to a ceramic serving bowl
made of clay

I scooped from the ground.

III

Rain falls, falling

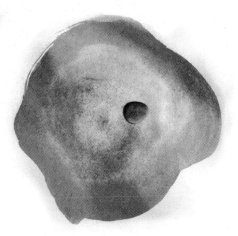

THIRTEEN ANTI-GHAZALS AFTER PHYLLIS WEBB

I

I didn't know the poet then.
A friend back from Salt Spring Island

told me she'd dropped off some books
to Phyllis Webb.

Phyllis, do you feel the world transforming?
This era of digital uniformity, pig-human hybridity.

In some parts of the world,
they are breeding monkeys with two heads.

One kitten whisker in a vault somewhere.
I have forgotten the combination.

How else to respond but to write as Webb?
I open a new deck of index cards.

Blue, pink, yellow.
Phyllis, did you write them on the front side

or the back?

*

II

An island fuses with the docks.
The wind blows all the poems into the water.

The poems scuba dive by themselves
closer to the narrow islands of Palawan.

To see the coral reefs, they say.
Before we swept the ocean confused with trawlers.

The whales here won't pose
for the locals. Just for the souvenir store.

At night, light guides the ferry to shore,
but there are other ways to get lost.

*

III

Sixty-two couplets at sundown
and sixty-two variations of the same couplet.

The last rainfall 'til September.

I get out of the rose garden
to tend to a less spiky bed of thorns.

The day hasn't got enough hours
for all the poems. To greet the sun, I assume.

The blackberry bush hides in a throng of blackbirds.
The shovel breaks for a midday beer.

*

IV

Art is perceived by the senses
in multiple dimensions. Rain falls, falling.

I've spent all morning trying to sound out—*wah*—
with a single intake of breath.

A line breaks off and reconnects,
Or it breaks off indefinitely.

Phyllis, I've poured myself, the sun,
and myself, to you.

I needn't a cassette player
in this day and age, Phyllis. Except to hear you.

*

v

I let the words fall on my lap—*Water and Light*
flips to where the page takes me.

Jupiter coughs up a memory
of last morning's dew.

There's not enough glow in all the sea's
twilight zone for me. Send some light down here!

The poems twist, entwine, orbit a serpentine loop
around Thursday's Canucks game.

The Great Wall of China soldiered
up the steps toward Monkey King heaven.

*

VI

I shut my eyes in the morning to welcome
the exoskeleton of a bug, the precision of its symmetry.

In some parts of the world, the folds of an origami swan
are judged by the textile design of its paper.

I have the interiority of a broken water painting
and the panes of a sliding glass door.

It's been a slow month for the little brown bat
escaping out an open window.

I leave the lights on for the moths,
but your found poems are nowhere to be found.

*

VII

The turning of leaves into yellow:
fall splits the tree in half.

October's last pollinators
line up for pumpkin spice honey.

Wah: try writing a ghazal
without pronouns.

At dawn, all the world's insect workers
spin cocoons over Rhys's fiction.

The poet refrains from writing.
Takes a caesura. Saltine and pears crumble.

*

The rain's persisted every day
of the month; busy, idlers on Hastings street.

One floor up from the seventies pint house,
the tin pots barge with a loud clang.

I found out who won the NBA finals
by the way my walls swayed.

Fists. Fists. Fists. Fists. Fists. They won't shut up.
Downstairs, the roar of fans. Blow horns in my studio.

Last night, there was a shooting here.
One more in the morning.

My ceiling board has a tune of its own
whenever someone makes love.

*

for John Thompson

Thompson, I catch a great big fish for you;
the trout, unresponsive as stone.

I know you know:
poetry isn't just in the song of the grieving.

So you are still here: the sky, the stove;
you've left me with no good recipe to follow.

When the days grow cold, I'll be responsible
for lighting my own poem; grove; trees.

After Ghalib,
I write in homage to all the women poets I know.

*

X

for Rita Wong

The caterpillar mistook my palm marks for a leaf,
where the folded gorge had been.

I run a finger along the topography
of your maps, your poems sketched out on real land.

Each day, I walk down a deserted railway
to the next shore. Eat coconut buns by the water.

Stand in a different spot every time the sea ends
and the land begins. You'll go to places.

All my friends, new to the West Coast:
the first thing they do is land, then go to the water.

*

What would you hang on a pegboard of the heart, Phyllis,
with all but one space remaining for your memories?

I have misplaced the night, comforted by the choir
of rice grains percussing at the bottom of a ceramic cooking pot.

Every meal has a provenance. Every evening spent alone
with a bowl of congee is memory-recall for the starving heart abroad.

Things I hunger for, Phyllis: spring onions, salted mustard tubers,
can't feed enough salt to the long memory

that will want to feed my grandmothers' generation—
stories of women who sculpted the imprint

of labour with their hands, and seasoned rice
with dried grains of their own sweat for salt and sustanance.

*

The poeting hand, an insomniac, disrupts the life cycle
of my potted plants in their REM sleep.

The string came loose.
The entire baby sock unravelled.

A lone squirrel, tempted by my freshly pruned shrubs
is curating its detailed acorn archive.

I am curating the recipe for next spring's garden:
indigos, day lilies, persimmons, forget-me-nots

that I'll surely forget for the hardships
of poeting in these coming winter months.

Ah, ah, ah—so harsh... I've planted flowers
Phyllis, so they may appear in future hours, and surprise me.

*

Sang is to sing a song in one language
and stone in another.

سنگ ها و صخره ها برای تو آواز میخوانند.
The stones sing for you, Phyllis.

I've travelled to the anchorage of sadness
in a night's dream; its song punctured me.

Winter stands between the tree
and its bare branches.

Phyllis, I tried to catch the kinesics
of your couplets in the trees.

*

IV

Hindsight

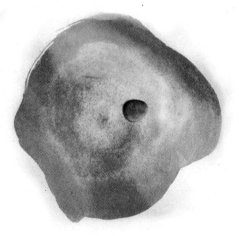

SUBCURRENT

Numbness is a temporary freedom from pain.

In the body are 37.2 trillion cells

that North American teenagers—like me—pretend

do not exist. The body as a vector converges

on multiple neuroses of the city,

where under the Vancouver Public Library

there is a holding cell for immigrant detainees.

And I struggle to think about the lives of children

in the world—love, and their parents

who love, know it in more human forms

than I've let subdue. Perhaps the truest

emotion then: to want to reciprocate

gently, beautifully for what one's taken

from the order of other living beings

to fulfill their animal needs. For some, the heart

will perish before it is forbidden to love.

HINDSIGHT

The decade's interlude leaves us in suspense
before the final act falls.

Spring goes on without us. The swallowtails
ripe out of their cocoons,

are eating our weight in misery
and growing too thin for the pendulum of the wind

carried with their wings by flight.

From behind private apartment walls, basement suites,
the cadence of children's footsteps

pass for May, June, July…

It's getting harder to believe
this month, that God doesn't exist

when I have so much still to ask for.
Can't tell in this night,

where we end and the universe begins.
I print out a picture of the sky

into a poem for her, so dark its edges disappear,
fall at the bottom of the inlet.

It will be months before Lao Lao receives it.
The woman writing to us in quarantine

will have run out of pages.

ON VISITING HABITAT ISLAND IN OLYMPIC VILLAGE
FOR THE FIRST TIME

The lights of your city are my lanterns
at night. I see the surface of your moon
weaving itself a new face
over the thread of ripples. Overhead
your dreams we all birthed,
your symphonies on the vaulted arch bridge
where you cooed yourself an infant
we rocked, hushed back to sleep. You know
the refrains of our lullabies
better than anyone: every music video
you possess delivers a sinew
of this extant summer's drum,
and the ecstasy of lovers
on high-rises and balconies,
while my own love is a Hudson's Bay away.

I arrived in the city by bus.
At first, I was the student and rain
was the conductor. The rain led me
home to the water radicals
on two characters of my Chinese name: 水—
these words
I've carried with me
for my entire life now spilling
spilling like

氵

氵

氵

For days,
I stooped at your transparent
avenues, cleansed fingers
and feet in sand, raised jujube berries
to Nan, never wanted to leave
your beaches. I've walked few shores
in my lifetime that have supported
my full weight in sinking.
So I let myself
fall deeper and deeper
to the gravity of your dispersing
        in warm
sand
that fell.

DRAMATIC MONOLOGUE

You wake me up in the night
to ask how strawberry the moon is
when the earth
is in decline.
        Outside the country
hungry artists
are turning fences
into an acrylic pouring
of the US–Mexico border.

*

Oil spills to the bottom
        of a fluorescent
lava lamp.
All my tinfoil sailboats
are sinking.

I live to see a day
when all the poems have been written
when the birds sing to us
in German
when they find a way to quarantine
        the earth with us,
our singing, and its light

back inside.

*

What if I am to be called Dave?
A tinfoil sailboat
set soaring by the different names of rain?
My mother cast me adrift
over too much water.

At dawn, I topped off
the edge
of a porcelain teacup.

*

You ask me why
I've not responded.
The seal
on an envelope
once broken

is like a scarred face.

IT'S BEEN WEEKS OF FOREST FIRES

It's been weeks without a poem
and you wonder how
you are still getting invited to readings.
Haven't they figured you out by now?

You bring the same year-old poems
and read until words that hurt
like the thorns of a blackberry
bush lose meaning.

Outside, sunflowers bobble upward
in advance. Wasps burrow inside
the flowering pods of figs that blossom
and soften in your neighbour's yard.

After days of eat and sleep,
sleep and eat, repeat,
you learn there are things
you can't numb away

and everything else fades.
Contents of late passing days you can't recall
except waking at two a.m.
to the chortle of crickets through sealed screens,

low hymn of mosquito melody,
the mild itch lining your arms and buttocks,
spreading like wildfire in the smoky haze.
The hue of the moon

turning bright red
as the blood you coughed up
chugging litres of sour kombucha
that doesn't suppress but stings like vodka.

Past the seawall, there are geese
riding waves under skies
that have turned the colour of the sea to muck
though it's not yet Halloween.

It's been weeks without rain.
The heirloom cherry tomatoes in your garden
burst and plummet
like dead mosquitoes against window ledge

in this summer more bountiful
than any you can harvest,
as lettuce leaves wilt, gnawed
by buzzing insect life: colonies of ants,
a bottle fly.

SPAWNING GROUNDS

1. Spawning Grounds

A female salmon by intuition returns to her prenatal stream carrying the weight of up to three thousand eggs. These, she will climb to deposit in the hollows of gravel and sediment above falls, packed between freshwater riverbeds but to be met along the way by the dam on Muskrat Falls off Labrador, the Keeyask Dam on the Nelson River, ninety-three square kilometres of hydro across boreal lands, snow forests liquefied where a common spawning ground resides for the wild fish being met with the Site C Dam through BC—128 kilometres of river flooded, the Peace River a reservoir, an Indigenous burial ground and home to one hundred endangered species. In the south, seventy-six killer whales left on the brink of extinction. We erect hydro dams and rear fish in hatcheries away from their natural habitat, bring wildlife back into Nature, Nature back into industrialization: this is what we call rewilding. The bare necessities of hatcheries strengthened through genetic engineering, forced interbreeding, but fish that rely on muscle memory year after year are the ones we see failing to return.

2. Shoreline

Sixty million cigarette butts currently clogging our oceans but we don't think of the watershed as a massive ashtray. More than plastic water bottles, more than straws, dislodged caps. And unlike plastic, filters can't be picked up. What's biodegradable disintegrates, what's disintegrated carries into rivers by rain. Arsenic, nicotine, lead into oceans. Watersheds evaporate, making a return to our bodies.

3. Sandcastle Bucket

A fable I grew up hearing told of a time when the sea swept to shore all its fishes. From the bluefin tuna off Scarborough to the mackerel migrating off-coast and what's left of wild sturgeon near Brescia, northern Italy. Where sinkholes had formed, where they were met with obstructions, and where the tide had begun to retreat, the fish could not get back. Along one shore, a child came with a sandcastle bucket, grabbed the fish by the handful and carried them back where they were released into the waters. This time, a bystander watched. They asked the child, *Why bother? There is so many of them.* To this, the child replied, *At least I'm doing something.* Hurry. The next time the sea turns again, there will be no more fish left to pick up.

4. Listen

A plastic bag pirouettes on the road. Watch how it heaves and falls in the air, clear as diatoms, like jellyfish in the water formation driven by the motors of vehicles pumping 250 mph, the wind blowing east and no one picks it up. Twenty-five plastic cups, a nylon sack and two flip-flops are not enough for conservation researchers to determine the cause of death, the sperm whale too decayed. A carcass washed ashore at Wakatobi National Park: a signal, as villagers read. *Come, butcher me.* So they do.

RITUAL FLOWERS

1. Sections of Being

The average person's torso holds

a mean segment weight that is 12.65% abdomen,

5.335% arm, that is 3.075% upper arm,

1.72% forearm, 0.575% hand, 14.81% pelvis,

18.56% thorax, 8.23% head,

that is 54.15% of the body together, 3.65%

of someone else's hand on my upper arm

—the squeeze, for condolences. 2166%

of the body that is the forty torsos

of my extended relatives knotted together at the funeral.

[ritual where | *"memory is the only relationship
we can have with the dead.* I'm sorry."

　　　—Leanne Dunic, *To Love the Coming End*]

A percentage too small every time

the tongue moves, delivers 100% of the heart—

the trembling swell, the expanding vernacular

of the thorax as it drowns

in an expressed percentage of the body's

repressed tears—the mean distribution

of the heart, each chamber not assigned

a percentage on the body statistical database.

2. Being Metaphors

["Power has no control over d

e   a

t

      h [...]

                Power no longer recognizes

                                    d

            e
            a   t

                      h.

Power literally ignores
d

e

            a

      t   h.   " —Foucault]

Death fell in petals on the funeral floor, made its way

to the podium for a speech. We left the flowers

scattered like ash like flakes of permanent snow

at our feet. Then, one by one family members

trickled out into their taxis and disappeared.

94

It's a cruel month for the dogwood to be bursting forth

white flowers, when some cultures believe

they are the colour of death. The funeral is a family

matter, until it becomes an individual sorrow. We mourn

only once together and will never show this grief

in public. No one raises death again. For a year,

no one dresses in white. Superstition is my country's

way of guarding against lost power to death

undermined by the colour of white as its end result.

Death becomes taboo, disguising bio-power's fear.

We discard clutches of white flowers

from our palms, hidden away in a private procession

of events / abandoned family album.

Overheard at the funeral:

I've spent all our money on her treatment and now

she is gone, and now, my daughter, we have nothing.

Memory of death betrays state power over life.

AUGUST

Everything's the same—

the silhouette of a city on the curtained wall,
cast by the uneven spines

of my books atop a shelf. The same
species of bird to visit the pruned hems

of my building's sage bush,
the same squirrel to excite my cat, plump

while coyotes roaming the tri-city margins
are ribbed and starving.

*

The Highland Way duplexes
lost an outdoor cat.

Then another one.

People begin bringing their cats in.

The coyotes are still hungry.

*

There's only so many
combinations of metaphors

you can make
with cupboard drawers

and indoor tropical plants.

*

The same emotions trigger
a good cry: yesterday, a young cougar

stalked a kid
and was euthanized.

Today, my roommate
told me she had a bonded ferret pair—

When one died, the other refused to eat,
followed in peaceful slumber.

*

Beauty's a memory of last summer, walking,
a passenger on the city shores.

Cloudless. Sunny.

I wished you were with me.
I wished the heron

and joggers and their cute sleeping babies
in strollers did not have to go unseen

or underappreciated by me.

*

The waterfront is the same these days, still radiant
and glowing, minus the August warmth,

minus friendly grins
tugging on the tight fabric masks

of strangers, still mouthing
their habitual *hello.*

*

A year of the same weekly
appointments, missed blood tests.

The doctor sends requisition after requisition
expired—efforts met by the words,

I'm so sorry.
I'll try harder, I promise.

A safety check each time the phone rings
from No Caller ID:

On a scale of one
to ten, how safe are you to yourself?

*

Breathe. The passing of the days /   /
expand /   / in a drift /   /

like tension /   / archived between
the body's /   / mitral valves.

Midnight and/   /fireworks.

*

Midnight measured/   /by the breath
of seven/   /to let in/   /another day.

*

OCCUPATIONAL HAZARD

I know the love and anguish of every man
    by the name of my father

        who drove himself to sleep every Sunday
            morning with alcohol, then drove himself

to the edge of the Yangtze River
    only to teach me to swim. No, Ba Ba,

        I know you. I know you never liked the taste
            of alcohol, but to put a roof over the idea

of your future daughter, you chose
    an occupation that required you to drink

        and drink as an elective. The night
            pouring out of bottles with cork tops

became the fog-dense morning in your head.
    The bubbles contained in fizzling

        champagne were stars that punctuated your breath,
            punctuated every broken syllable

you tried to conceal from your family in the ER.
    Ba Ba, what else have you

        given up for me? *How many days does he have to go*
            on entertaining clients? Mother would say.

The life of a businessman is an occupational hazard
      that dissolves the Ba Ba I had

             in all my previous photographs of you
                   into postcards with foreign stamps

from Thailand, Amsterdam, places
      where the stores with postcards

             had closed so you mailed me their airport brochures.
                   Mother couldn't understand why I stole the socks

from your undergarments drawer
      and slept with your dirty laundry,

             mistaking my missing you for her young daughter wanting to
                   have inappropriate relations with men.

But you were the only man
      I've ever loved as a daughter—

             Once, I begged you to take me with you
               on a business trip to Qufu—

woke up to the sight of you
      intoxicated on the hotel room floor.

             Quickly, you say.
               Ba Ba slipped and cracked

his shin over the toilet-bowl rim. It hurts so bad.
      Quickly daughter, call the concierge. I picked up

the telephone and asked for four
            Band-Aids please, the way a five-year-old

can stare upon the deep gorge of the human body
        and not be scared, for she recognizes the bone

            as her Ba Ba's sacrifice glistening under light and blood
                as if to say, *One day, daughter,*

I'll have saved to buy you a future
        that is shiny. And the four Band-Aids

            she has to offer in return for her father's love
                will be both enough and not enough, eternally.

How can I ever repay you? How can I spare your heart
        of breaking? The heart of a businessman

            sells investments for a living
                and the heart of a writer invests in living.

But I could not inform the world of your love
        otherwise—don't be disappointed anymore.

            I miss you Ba Ba, and your voice
                on the receiving line is nowhere to be heard.

SERENADE NO. I IN SUNFLOWERS

for Scout Ruppe

Children are born with the circadian rhythm of sunflowers.
When they laugh, their eyes dot the distance

between noon and night,

turn to where the sun shines brightest. Their arms are like hovercrafts,
outstretched toward the simplest things: a morsel of sunflower jelly,
     and sun butter.

*

Light is a matter not taught   for those blessed
with the heads of a thousand tiny flowers

and the inflorescence of tears

to make the whole world pure,
though some never learn to repress this.

*

Blow into your hand the petals
of the different hues and you will see the sky

in pink, rouge, terracotta gold—

the sunset you and I have created from blooms.

*

Tournesol is a French word meaning to turn with the sun,
and *une lumière perdue*, a lost light.

To find it again, kneel at a child's eye level and look, really look.

Focus in closely
on what they are trying to show you.

*

Because one doesn't have to be made of glass to let light in...

*

Those who came before us, left with a graft of your stalk
to plant for another season
walked for miles on gravel
only to be replaced by the weight of walking

and sand that, having absorbed the intensity of stars, now makes up
   the desert.

*

The average sunflower takes sixty to eighty-five days to pollinate.
One hundred days to grow seeds.
Only young flowers move; only young flowers have to.

The mature wait for bees to come to them.

Do they ever berate themselves the way we do upon leaving,
a measure of time that some call the West, and some call serendipity

never being able to look back?

*

The sun fits 960,000 earths at its core. That's 1.969×10^9 sunflowers per
    square mile on earth.
1.89024×10^{14} seeds I would plant with you.

For every bird, and every person grieving.

*

If I gave you a seed, would you promise to throw it away
so that it has a chance to make the world better?

Because some gifts are not meant for hanging on to.

Because we'll have many more years to stain the grass fields yellow.

*

Because the word *because* is a beautiful word
you once used to explain to me why sunflowers are your favourite flower.

When you smile, you make the world bloom with the faces of sunflowers

for the people who hurt you
and love you the same.

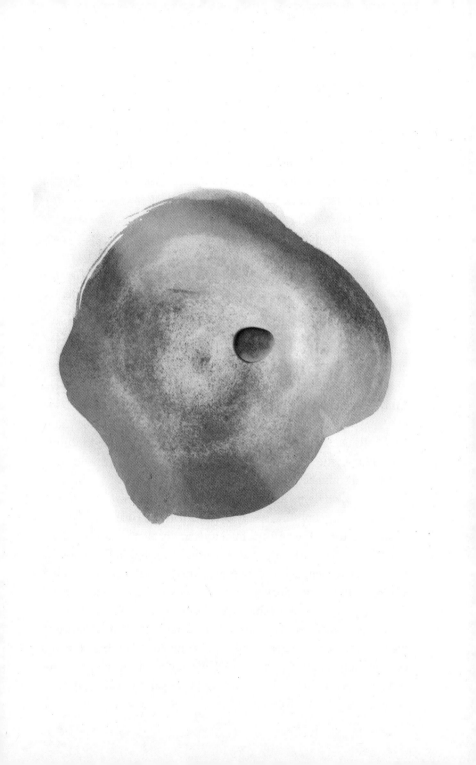

ACKNOWLEDGEMENTS

Thank you to Silas White, Emma Skagen and the entire team at Nightwood Editions.

Earlier versions of poems in this collection have appeared in *Room, Looseleaf, Train, The Temz Review, Wordworks, Plenitude, Canthius, Contemporary Verse 2, Geez Magazine, The Lyre, Minola Review, Chaudiere Books, The Puritan, Prairie Fire, Grain, Arc Poetry Magazine, The Fiddlehead, PRISM International* and *Canadian Literature.* The poem "Spawning Grounds" has also appeared in the anthologies *Watch Your Head* (Coach House Books, 2020, edited by Kathryn Mockler) and *They Rise Like a Wave* (Blue Oak Press, 2021, edited by Christine Kitano and Alycia Pirmohamed).

An early handful of the poems in this book were composed in my last year of high school with the support of many of my teachers. These poems sprung out of the poetry workshops I was taking through SFU's Continuing Studies under the generous mentorship of Fiona Tinwei Lam, Evelyn Lau and Rob Taylor. These poems grew into a chapbook, *On Forgetting a Language*, published by Baseline Press. Thank you to my publisher, Karen Schindler. I am forever indebted to your intuitive edits, support, those wonderful hours carefully discussing poetry over coffee, and your beautiful handwritten notes in the mail.

More gratitude to the following: Mark Deggan—your deep wisdom and always uplifting spirit; jokes I can depend on. Thank you for being invested in the beauty of poetry and my alter ego, Dave. Melek Ortabasi for the nurturing spaces you have created in the world literature department and lasting friendships in your classrooms. Lindsey Freeman for introducing me to the world of sociological poetry, for your guidance and invaluable feedback on the project-in-progress which spurred current versions of "Subcurrent" and "Ritual Flowers." Ivan Coyote, Carleigh Baker and Otoniya Juliane Okot Bitek for your consultations and feedback, and each of your beautiful energies while serving as Writer in Residence for the SFU Department of English.

A deep thank you to Stephen Collis for your care, contagious enthusiasm and editorial feedback on this manuscript. And for leading me to ghazals and Phyllis Webb.

Thank you to Diana Solomon, Erik Christensen and Abby—caring, beautiful presences who've become very important to me.

Zoë Dagneault and Violet, for autumn memories; sunflower and tulip memories. Walking Bello and Sunny memories.

Catherine and Richard, for found families.

And to my dear friend, Natalie Lim, an anchoring presence and collaborator. Thank you for inspiring me with your poems and providing your thoughtful feedback on parts of this manuscript. My best friend since grade ten, Mia Kartodirdjo, for being in my life, and for being you. LJ Weisberg, for Scrabble on the seventh floor of the library and our many mutual interests, mostly over cat-related things. Chimedum Ohaegbu for countless moments shared at readings and meetups. Nedda Sarshar, for those hours that just pass by with you when we are discussing writing and Iranian poetry. Izzy and Sarah, for turning off the stove when I've wandered off to write some new poem thingy.

My many friends who've taken time out of their schedules to meet up and spoil me with bookstore visits and food every time I find myself in Ontario. Thank you to the Growing Room Collective. My friends from near and far. To the community, for showing me immense kindness and support from day one.

My kitten, Dany Loki Chaos. My love, Scout. I didn't know I had happy poems in me until I met you.

PHOTO CREDIT: ZOË DAGNEAULT

ABOUT THE AUTHOR

Isabella Wang is the author of the chapbook *On Forgetting a Language* (Baseline Press, 2019). She has been shortlisted for *Arc Poetry Magazine's* Poem of the Year Contest, *The Malahat Review*'s Far Horizons Award for Poetry and Long Poem Contest, *Minola Review*'s Poetry Contest, and was the youngest writer to be shortlisted twice for *The New Quarterly*'s Edna Staebler Personal Essay Contest. Wang's poetry and prose have appeared in over thirty literary journals and three anthologies, including *Watch Your Head: Writers and Artists Respond to the Climate Crisis* (Coach House Books, 2020) and *They Rise Like a Wave: An Anthology of Asian American Women Poets* (Blue Oak Press, 2021). She studies English and world literature at Simon Fraser University, and is an editor at *Room* magazine. *Pebble Swing* is her debut full-length collection.